DEADLY CREATURES

Coloring Book

JAN SOVAK

Dover Publications, Inc.
Mineola, New York

NOTE

Not all animals are cute and cuddly. Nature comes in many forms—venomous snakes, roaring lions, and sharks with razor-sharp teeth included. But remember, the deadliest animals aren't always the ones with the sharpest teeth, or the biggest claws! Did you know that the little poison dart frog, only about two inches long, contains enough venom to kill ten adult human beings? Or that elephants in Africa and India often invade and trample human villages? All of these, plus a host of others, can all be found inside this coloring book. Featuring 30 scientifically accurate, black-and-white renderings of deadly animals, plus brief captions detailing what each is infamous for—this book is not for the faint of heart!

Copyright

Copyright © 2011 by Dover Publications, Inc.
All rights reserved.

Bibliographical Note

Deadly Creatures Coloring Book is a new work, first published by Dover Publications, Inc., in 2011.

International Standard Book Number

ISBN-13: 978-0-486-47655-1
ISBN-10: 0-486-47655-3

Manufactured in the United States by Courier Corporation
47655301
www.doverpublications.com

The **sea wasp** or **marine stinger jellyfish** can produce enough venom in a single sting to kill about 60 humans. It lives off the coast of Australia, and sometimes injures swimmers who have accidentally bumped into its long tentacles.

This venomous species of sea snail looks harmless, but beware! A sting from the **textile cone** is excruciatingly painful, and can easily kill a human being if not treated quickly. Textile cones live on coral reefs, and scuba divers usually fear these little snails more than sharks!

The **blue-ringed octopus** is tiny—only about the size of a golf ball—but its venom can kill a human adult in less than ten minutes. There is no known anti-venom for a blue ringed octopus bite, and the only way a victim can survive is get medical attention fast and to be placed on a ventilator until the venom runs through their system.

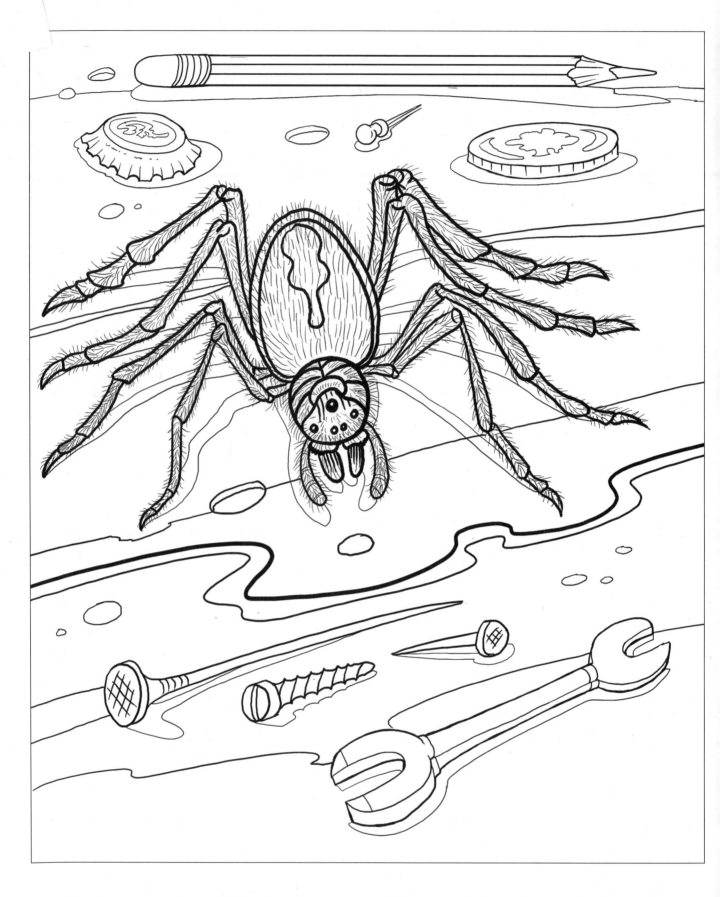

The **brown recluse spider** threatens human beings much more frequently than other venomous creatures, since it tends to live inside people's homes, in dark corners and crevices, and inside seldom-worn clothing or curtains. Although the brown recluse's bite isn't deadly, it causes a large and extremely painful wound on the skin, and can take months to heal.

Scorpions are small creatures that live in deserts and tropical regions all over the world. Although they rarely kill human beings, the scorpion's sting is extremely painful, and causes nausea, convulsions, and sometimes coma.

The **giant hornet** can grow to be about the size of a human hand, and can fly at speeds up to 25 miles per hour! It is very aggressive when disturbed and has been known to sting its victim multiple times.

The **giant stingray** lives in the freshwater bodies of Southeast Asia. It is one of the world's largest fishes, weighing over 1,000 pounds! Its size alone makes this creature a danger to humans, but its poisonous, barbed tail is an even larger threat.

Not only is the **bull shark** the most likely shark to attack a human being, but it prefers shallow, coastal waters as its habitat—the same waters where humans like to swim. These aggressive predators will eat almost anything they can close their jaws on!

The aggressive **great white shark** has earned itself the nickname "man killer." In fact, several hundred great white shark attacks worldwide are reported yearly. This giant shark, which can reach lengths of up to 15 feet, can be found off the coast of every continent except Antarctica.

The **stonefish** is well camouflaged under water, its bumpy, brown skin resembling a stone. It has a row of spines running along its back that remain hidden in its flesh until the stonefish feels threatened, upon which they shoot up and inject venom into the offending sea creature—or human foot!

The little **poison dart frog,** which grows to be only about two inches long, contains enough venom to kill ten adult humans. However, poison dart frogs rarely kill, as its venom is secreted out of the skin, and is only dangerous if brought into contact with the mouth.

The **komodo dragon,** the world's largest lizard, can smell its prey from as far as 5 miles away. Komodos are not picky eaters, and will eat anything from pigs and deer, to water buffalo, other komodos, and occasionally, human intruders.

The giant **black mamba** snake can grow to be up to 14 feet long. It is also very fast, slithering at a speed of about 12 miles per hour. Mambas deliver their venom by a set of hollow fangs, and a bite can easily kill a human if left untreated.

The **king cobra** is the largest venomous snake in the world, reaching lengths of about 18 feet long. It is the most feared and dangerous snake in Asia, and a single bite from the king cobra can kill a human in about 30 minutes if left untreated.

The **spitting cobra** has the ability to eject venom from its fangs when it feels threatened. The venom is generally harmless if it comes in contact with the skin, but causes blindness if it gets in the eyes.

The **barba amarilla** or **"yellow beard"** snake lives in Central and South America, and is known to frequently bite humans (or anything else) that accidentally gets in its way. Aggressive and easily agitated, the barba amarilla will usually raise its head high in the air in order to strike, often resulting in bites higher than the knee.

Although the **python** is not venomous, its size alone makes it quite dangerous. It holds the record for the longest snake ever measured, with one specimen recorded at 33 feet long.

Crocodiles are very dangerous to humans. Not only are they large, and powerful, and willing to chase their prey a considerable distance, but more often than not they strike before the victim has time to react.

The **hyena** is the most common large carnivore in Africa. Both a powerful hunter and a scavenger, the hyena will eat anything from live or dead animals and other hyenas, to bones and droppings.

19

Often exceeding 550 pounds, the **lion** is both a powerful and an aggressive hunter. They live in large packs, and several lions will often hunt together. Although they can reach speeds of up to 50 miles per hour, they usually prefer to stalk and sneak up on their prey.

The largest of the big cats, the **tiger** can weigh up to 660 pounds, with teeth measuring about 4 inches. They generally prefer to hunt alone and, like the lion, would rather stalk their prey than chase it. Although healthy tigers usually avoid humans, old or infirm tigers have been known to invade villages.

Cougars are large and slender animals, with the ability to jump over 16 feet high and run at speeds reaching up to 40 miles per hour. Like most cats, they prefer to stalk their prey rather than chase it.

The **grizzly bear** is at the top of the food chain, hunted only occasionally by wolf packs and humans. Despite its strength and large size, the grizzly prefers nuts, berries, fish, fruit, and roots to larger game. However, mother grizzlies are very protective of their cubs, and will attack intruders.

The **hippopotamus** is the third largest land mammal, and is mostly herbivorous. Despite its harmless and even goofy appearance, African experts consider the hippo one of the most dangerous animals on the continent. They often upset boats, and bite without being provoked.

Native to Africa and Asia, the **rhinoceros,** like the hippo, is generally a non-violent herbivore, but is known for episodes of unprovoked aggression. The rhino has very poor eyesight and it is likely that it perceives any unfamiliar intruder as cause for alarm.

Despite its gentle, lumbering appearance, the **elephant,** which can weigh up to 20,000 pounds, can easily crush any other land animal. In Africa and India, there are frequent reports of elephants invading and destroying human villages.

Another surprisingly aggressive herbivore, the **moose** is a very nervous animal, and will often charge at human intruders, and especially at dogs. A female moose, called a cow, will become aggressive when she feels protective of her young.

Buffalo or **bison** are herbivores that roam together in large herds. They are unlikely to attack under normal circumstances, but are relentless if provoked. Because of their large body size they appear slow, but can actually run at speeds up to 35 miles per hour.

The **piranha** is an omnivorous species of fish with a well-deserved reputation for its sharp teeth and preference for meat. Although their small size makes them a very minor threat to humans, they sometimes injure incautious swimmers.

The **wolf** is a powerful hunter who usually roams with a small pack. The wolf is near the top of the food chain, with only humans and tigers as its predators. It will often chase its prey for long distances before striking, slowly wearing it out.